Dream BIG American Idol SUPERSTARS

Kris Allen

David Archuleta **DISCARD**

Kelly Clarkson

David Cook

Chris Daughtry

Jennifer Hudson

Adam Lambert

Kellie Pickler

Jordin Sparks

Carrie Underwood

Elliott Yamin

American Idol Profiles Index:
Top Finalists from Seasons 1 to 7
(82 Contestants)

Insights Into American Idol

Jennifer Hudson

Gail Snyder

Mason Crest Publishers

Produced by 21st Century Publishing and Communications, Inc.

MASON CREST PUBLISHERS INC.
370 Reed Road
Broomall, Pennsylvania 19008
(866) MCP-BOOK (toll free)
www.masoncrest.com

Printed in the United States of America.

First Printing

9 8 7 6 5 4 3 2 1

Library of Congress Cataloging-in-Publication Data

Snyder, Gail.
    Jennifer Hudson / Gail Snyder.
        p. cm. — (Dream big: American Idol superstars)
    Includes bibliographical references and index.
    ISBN 978-1-4222-1509-8 (hardback : alk. paper)
    ISBN 978-1-4222-1601-9 (pbk. : alk. paper)
    1. Hudson, Jennifer, 1981–   —Juvenile literature. 2. Singers—United States—
Biography—Juvenile literature. 3. Motion picture actors and actresses—United
States—Biography—Juvenile literature. I. Title.
    ML3930.H82S69 2010
    782.42164092—dc22
    [B]   2009021192

CONTENTS

American Idol TIMELINE

October 5, 2001
Pop Idol, a TV reality show created by Simon Fuller, debuts in the United Kingdom and becomes a smash hit.

Fall 2001
Based on the success of *Pop Idol*, and after initially rejecting the concept, FOX Network agrees to buy *American Idol*, a national talent competition and TV reality show.

Spring 2002
Auditions for *American Idol* Season 1 are held in New York City, Los Angeles, Chicago, Dallas, Miami, Atlanta, and Seattle.

January 21, 2003
American Idol Season 2 premieres without Brian Dunkleman, leaving Ryan Seacrest as the sole host.

May 21, 2003
- *American Idol* Season 2 finale airs.
- Ruben Studdard narrowly wins and Clay Aiken is the runner-up.
- Runner-up Clay Aiken goes on to become extremely successful both critically and commercially.

January 19, 2004
American Idol Season 3 premieres.

2001 **2002** **2003** **2004**

June 11, 2002
American Idol Season 1 premieres on FOX Network, with Simon Cowell, Paula Abdul, and Randy Jackson as the judges, and Ryan Seacrest and Brian Dunkleman as the co-hosts.

September 4, 2002
- *American Idol* Season 1 finale airs.
- Kelly Clarkson wins and Justin Guarini is the runner-up.
- Kelly Clarkson goes on to become the most successful Idol winner and a superstar in the music industry.

Fall 2002
Auditions for *American Idol* Season 2 are held in New York City, Los Angeles, Miami, Detroit, Nashville, and Austin.

January 27, 2004
William Hung's audition is aired and his humble response to Simon Cowell's scathing criticism make William the most famous American Idol non-qualifier and earn him record deals and a cult-like following.

April 21, 2004
Jennifer Hudson is voted off the show in 7th place, and goes on to win the role of Effie in *Dreamgirls*, for which she wins an Academy Award, a Golden Globe Award, and a Grammy Award.

May 26, 2004
- *American Idol* Season 3 finale airs with 65 million viewers casting their votes.
- Fantasia Barrino is crowned the winner and Diana DeGarmo is the runner-up.
- Fantasia soon becomes the first artist in the history of Billboard to debut at number one with her first single.

May 10, 2006
Chris Daughtry is voted off the show in 4th place, and soon after forms the band, Daughtry, and releases its debut album, which becomes number one on the charts, wins many awards, and finds huge commercial success.

April 26, 2006
Kellie Pickler is voted off the show in 6th place, and soon releases her debut album, which rockets to number one on the Billboard Top Country Album chart.

January 17, 2006
American Idol Season 5 premieres and for the first time airs in high definition.

May 24, 2006
- *American Idol* Season 5 finale airs.
- Taylor Hicks is the winner and Katharine McPhee the runner-up.
- Elliot Yamin, the second runner-up, goes on to release his debut album, which goes gold.

January 16, 2007
American Idol Season 6 premieres.

April 2007
The *American Idol* Songwriting Contest is announced.

January 15, 2008
American Idol Season 7 airs with a four-hour two-day premiere.

April 9, 2008
Idol Gives Back returns for its second year.

May 21, 2008
- *American Idol* Season 7 finale airs.
- David Cook wins with 54.6 million votes and David Archuleta is the runner-up with 42.9 million votes.
- Both Davids go on to tremendous post-Idol success with successful albums and singles.

2005   2006   2007   2008   2009

May 25, 2005
- *American Idol* Season 4 finale airs.
- Carrie Underwood wins and Bo Bice is the runner-up.
- Carrie goes on to become one of the most successful Idol winners, selling millions of albums and winning scores of major awards.

January 18, 2005
- *American Idol* Season 4 premieres.
- Some rules change:
  - The age limit is raised from 24 to 28.
  - The semi-final competition is separated by gender up until the 12 finalists.

April 24–25, 2007
American Idol Gives Back, a charitable campaign to raise money for underprivileged children worldwide, airs, and raises more than $70 million.

May 23, 2007
- *American Idol* Season 6 finale airs.
- Jordin Sparks wins with 74 million votes and Blake Lewis is the runner-up.
- Jordin goes on to join Kelly Clarkson and Carrie Underwood in the ranks of highly successful post-Idol recording artists.

January 13, 2009
American Idol Season 8 premieres adding Kara DioGuardi as a fourth judge.

February 14, 2009
The American Idol Experience, a theme park attraction, officially opens at Disney's Hollywood Studio in Florida.

May 20, 2009
- *American Idol* Season 8 finale airs.
- Kris Allen unexpectedly wins and Adam Lambert is the runner-up.
- Almost 100 million people voted in the season 8 finale.

Jennifer Hudson confidently takes her place on the red carpet at the 79th Academy Awards, February 25, 2007. That night she won an Oscar for Best Supporting Actress for her show-stopping performance in *Dreamgirls*. After having been voted off *American Idol*, Jennifer went on to become only the third African-American woman to win an Academy Award; she indeed has arrived.

1

She Has Arrived

As she sat in the audience at the Kodak Theater in Hollywood on February 25, 2007, watching as the Academy Awards ceremony unfolded around her, singer and actress Jennifer Hudson was not at all certain she would win the Oscar for Best Supporting Actress for her first-ever role in the movie *Dreamgirls*.

Despite the buzz that surrounded her role as Effie White in the movie—the same role that had made the career of Jennifer's idol, Jennifer Holliday, in the **Broadway** play—Hudson was mindful that most of her competitors were far more experienced actresses. She was awed to be in the same company as Adriana Barraza and Rinko Kikuchi, both nominated for *Babel*, and Cate Blanchett, for *Notes on a Scandal*.

In fact, the then 24-year-old with the larger than life **soprano** voice had been thrilled just to receive so much pre-Oscar attention as a member of an all-star cast that included Jamie Foxx, Eddie Murphy, and Beyoncé. Jennifer said,

> **It's the biggest honor I could possibly get. I'm so grateful. All I wanted was the part, and to hear this now? It's very exciting.**

Teary-Eyed and Speechless

Still, by the time Oscar night rolled around Jennifer had already won a Golden Globe Award for her show-stopping role as Effie, a big-boned **rhythm and blues** singer who fights back after she gets muscled out of a singing group and loses her boyfriend to another, more conventionally pretty member of the group.

Even though she had already given one acceptance speech when she picked up the Golden Globe—often an indicator of an impending Oscar—when Jennifer heard her name announced as winner at the Academy Awards she was teary-eyed and speechless.

Clad in a sparkling gown designed by Oscar de La Renta and standing before an audience filled with the most important people in the movie industry, Jennifer begged for a moment to collect her thoughts. She said,

> **I didn't think I was going to win but, wow, if my grandmother was here to see me now. She was my biggest inspiration for everything because she was a singer and she had the passion for it but she never had the chance. And that was the thing that pushed me forward to continue.**

After the Oscar show ended Jennifer chose not to attend any of the post-show parties. A churchgoer who got her start singing gospel music as a small child, Jennifer preferred a much quieter form of celebration. She told a reporter,

"I just went back to my room and sat with the Oscar. . . . I remember after I won it, I asked director Bill Condon, 'Can they take it back?'"

Adored by Fans and Critics

Although she had been considered a favorite for the Oscar, Jennifer could not forget that her dream had been deferred once before. She was voted off *American Idol* in the show's third season, even though the judges largely loved her give-it-everything-she-has delivery of the songs she performed.

Jennifer poses with her Oscar for Best Supporting Actress for her outstanding performance as Effie in *Dreamgirls*. In her emotional acceptance speech, Jennifer remembered her grandmother, who inspired her to fulfill her dream to be a singer.

That adoration carried over to movie **critics** like the one for the *Los Angeles Times* who wrote that Jennifer "not only owns the movie, she rides it like a rocket to instant stardom." And a *New York Times* writer gushed,

> **"It's not often you go to the movies and see a big-boned, sexually assertive, self-confident black woman—not played for laughs or impersonated by a male comedian in drag—holding the middle of the screen. And when was the last time you saw a first-time film actress upstage an Oscar winner (Jamie Foxx), a pop diva (Beyoncé) and a movie star (Eddie Murphy) of long standing? Ms. Hudson is not going anywhere. She has arrived."**

FAMOUS "LOSERS"

American Idol has launched the successful careers of several singers who, like Jennifer Hudson, didn't win the competition but nevertheless won the hearts of the American public.

Clay Aiken, who was runner up in *Idol*'s second season, gained critical attention for his role as Lancelot in the Broadway musical *Spamalot,* and his album sales have outpaced those of other male *Idol* vocalists.

Chris Daughtry of season five is the next most successful male artist with *Idol* ties. His rock band Daughtry produced one of the biggest rock albums of 2006.

Thanks to his legions of dedicated fans, Elliott Yamin, season five's second runner-up, saw his self-titled first album climb to the top spot for independent albums in 2007, according to *Billboard* magazine.

Multi-Award Winner

In a poll conducted by *USA Today* shortly after the Academy Awards, 61 percent of adults echoed the critics by revealing that

Jennifer (right), Oscar winner for Best Supporting Actress, and costar Beyoncé share a memorable duet, "Love You I Do," from *Dreamgirls* at the 2007 Academy Awards. Jennifer had come a long way since being voted off *American Idol,* and critics were now praising her as an actress who was rocketing to stardom.

they too had a good opinion of Jennifer. Fifty-seven percent of those surveyed also said that Jennifer was likely to have a long, successful career.

In addition to the Oscar statue, which sits in a prominent spot on Jennifer's mantel at home, she won numerous other awards for *Dreamgirls.* She was also recognized by the Screen Actors Guild, the British Academy of Film and Television Arts, and the Broadcast Film Critic's Association, and received a NAACP Image Award and Soul Train Entertainer of the Year Award. She has acknowledged that none of those accolades would have been possible if she had not first stepped onto the stage of *American Idol* two years before.

Jennifer's earliest singing experience came in church one day when her mother took her to choir practice. Although only a toddler, Jennifer surprised everyone by enthusiastically singing a high note that grownups were struggling to reach.

2

Born to Sing

Jennifer Kate Hudson was born September 12, 1981, in Chicago, Illinois, into a loving, churchgoing African-American family. According to a family legend, when Jennifer was a baby her mother took her to a choir practice. There, some of the choir members were struggling with a note but, to everyone's amazement, baby Jennifer hit it perfectly.

Jennifer grew up in a tough part of the city. Her mother, Darnell, was a secretary, and Jennifer's stepfather, Samuel Simpson, drove a bus to support the family, which also included an older sister Julia, a brother Jason, and three stepsiblings.

Although money was tight, the family still had enough of it for Jennifer to take ballet lessons. Her sister Julia recalls,

> **"When we were little girls, I was the tomboy, but she wanted style. When we could afford it, our mother took us to buy clothes and let us pick. I wanted pants. Jennifer always wanted the frilly skirt."**

Following in Grandma's Footsteps

One of the places in which Jennifer felt most at home was Pleasant Gift Missionary Baptist Church, where she first sang in the choir

At an early age, Jennifer loved to sing solos at church. She lovingly credits her grandmother, who was also in the choir, as the source of her inspiration, singing talent, and her ability to put emotion into her songs.

when she was seven years old. That is where she developed a talent for singing solos. Her grandmother, Julia Kate Hudson, for whom Jennifer is named, was a **church elder** and choir member. She was Jennifer's first musical influence. Jennifer said,

> **❝They say I got my voice from my grand-mother. She just wanted to sing for the Lord in church. That's part of where I got my emotion from. I would hear her voice singing, 'How Great Thou Art.'❞**

BORROWING FROM WHITNEY HOUSTON

As Jennifer grew older she began to relate to other singers besides her grandmother. Whitney Houston became a particular favorite. Whitney's full gospel voice produced hit after hit when Jennifer was growing up, and her single, "I Will Always Love You," was among the biggest in the history of rock 'n' roll. During her *American Idol* competition, Jennifer reached into Whitney's song book to sing "I Believe in You and Me," the song that brought her back as a wild card after she had previously been voted off the show.

Jennifer soon found many more opportunities to sing for audiences at weddings, baptisms, and funerals. At Paul Laurence Dunbar Vocational Career Academy, the high school she attended, Jennifer was a member of the chorus. She confidently told the chorus director,

> **❝I'm going to make you proud of me. I'm going to be a famous singer.❞**

Her first paying job was at the local Burger King, a position she obtained at 16. She often worked at the drive-in window but did not really enjoy the work. Meanwhile, her talent as a singer was becoming obvious to others as her fellow high school students named her "most talented" in her senior year.

IDOLIZING ARETHA

Known as Lady Soul, Aretha Franklin's big voice has influenced countless rhythm and blues singers with such signature songs as "Respect," "Think," and "Chain of Fools." Franklin appeared in *The Blues Brothers* movie and her music has been part of the soundtrack for other films like *Legally Blond 2* and *Bridget Jones's Diary.*

Like Jennifer, Franklin got her start singing in church. Jennifer chose a Franklin song for her *Idol* audition. Her performance of "Share Your Love with Me" was more than good enough to guarantee a place on the show. Judge Randy Jackson said her cover of the song was "absolutely brilliant."

When Jennifer was 17 years old her grandmother died. It was a terrible blow to Jennifer because grandmother Julia was the person who was most supportive of her singing. Within a year her stepfather also died. Losing two close relatives at such a young age was hard, but Jennifer's relationship with her church was a comfort.

First Professional Job

In 2001, Jennifer briefly attended two different colleges, one in Oklahoma that made her feel homesick, and another in her hometown. While studying music at Kennedy-King College in Chicago she auditioned for and received a role in the musical *Big River.* Jennifer's solo in the play, a musical adaptation of *The Adventures of Huckleberry Finn,* was so full of emotion that audience members were brought to tears at nearly every performance. Written by Mark Twain, *Huckleberry Finn* is the story of a young 19th century runaway boy's adventures on the Mississippi River.

Her next job also involved water: Jennifer found work on a Disney cruise ship as the singing narrator in a musical adaptation of *Hercules.* She said,

Aretha Franklin is a rhythm and blues singer known as Lady Soul. She began her career singing in church and has influenced countless singers over the years. In her *Idol* audition, Jennifer impressed the judges enough with her soulful rendition of one of Aretha's songs to move on to the next round.

“To be able to sing for 8,000 people a week is amazing. It's like, 'Are you serious? You're paying me to do this?' It was very exciting.”

Although she enjoyed working on the cruise ship, when her mother suggested Jennifer audition for *American Idol* she gave the idea careful consideration before deciding to try out. Like everyone else who watched the first two seasons of the popular television program, Jennifer knew that *Idol* could make her a star and she could not wait for her turn to shine.

Jennifer always gives it her all when she performs during the *Idol* competition. Her *Idol* journey was not easy; she was eliminated, came back in the wild card round, and was eventually voted off in 6th place. But Jennifer's faith was strong and she always had hope, never gave up, and often got great reviews from the judges.

3

Blowing Away Elton John

By the time Jennifer took an airplane to Atlanta, Georgia, to audition for *American Idol* in August 2003, the show had already elevated Kelly Clarkson, Ruben Studdard, and Clay Aiken to international music stars. She had little doubt that waiting among the thousands of hopefuls gathered at the Georgia Dome in Atlanta could lead to good things.

The atmosphere at the Georgia Dome resembled a big party to which thousands of people had been invited. Jennifer was among the hopefuls who camped out, bringing with them all the things they needed to be comfortable, like sleeping bags, air mattresses, books, games, and food. It was a great opportunity to meet other aspiring singers while everybody prepared and waited for their auditions.

Jennifer recalled her earliest audition:

> **"They wanted an original song but I didn't have one so I did this kinda obscure song, 'This Empty Place,' that I first heard performed by Cissy Houston. Then the judges wanted to hear something they knew so I did Celine Dion's 'Power of Love' and then 'Survivor' by Destiny's Child."**

Similar auditions were also held in New York, Houston, Los Angeles, San Francisco, and Honolulu. In all, 70,000 people got their chance to sing before *American Idol* producers involved in the screening process. Only a small number of promising

WHO ARE THE JUDGES?

British-born Simon Cowell is one of the most powerful record executives in the country. Yet he admits that he doesn't sing, can barely play the guitar, and doesn't produce albums. He is good, however, at finding talented recording artists who can make money for the *American Idol* franchise and Sony/BMG, the record company he works for. Ordinary people come up to him on the street and beg him to judge them.

Unlike Simon, New Orleans native and *Idol* judge Randy Jackson plays bass and was a member of the rock group Journey. He, too, is experienced at signing new musical groups for major record labels. He has worked closely with Madonna and Destiny's Child and has had a hand in the creation of a thousand gold and multiplatinum albums.

No one could identify more with aspiring singers than Paula Abdul, a Grammy Award–winning California singer with more than 30 million record sales to her credit. Paula has also earned fame as a choreographer for Janet Jackson and other artists who used her talents to create their music videos.

In season eight, a second woman judge was added. She is Kara DioGuardi, a prolific songwriter from New York who has written for Clay Aiken, Kelly Clarkson, and Carrie Underwood. Others who have recorded her songs include the Jonas Brothers, Pink, and Britney Spears.

American Idol judges (from left) Randy Jackson, Paula Abdul, and Simon Cowell hold auditions in cities across America in the weeks before the televised series. Their decision to send a competitor to Hollywood can lead to a life-changing break into a music career.

candidates actually sang in front of the famous *American Idol* judges: record executive Randy Jackson, Grammy-winning singer and celebrity Paula Abdul and acid-tongued Simon Cowell, who is part-owner of the program and provides much of the drama with his frequently devastating put-downs of singers' performances and clothing choices.

Singing Her Behind Off

Jennifer made it through the initial screening, earning the right to sing for judges Randy, Paula, and Simon. Wearing a black dress with spaghetti straps that were falling down as she moved her expressive arms, Jennifer calmly sang Aretha Franklin's "Share Your Love with Me." It was a performance that pleased all three judges. Randy said, "The best singer I've heard so far; brilliant." Added Paula, "No doubt about it, you can sing your behind off."

Told that she had made it onto the show, Jennifer left the audition room and sang the news to her family members waiting outside: "I'm going to Hollywood!" She was one of just 116 contestants to advance to the next level of competition in which the judges whittle down the number of aspiring singers to 32.

Her filmed audition in front of the *Idol* judges aired on television on February 2, 2004. That was the night America met Jennifer and got its first opportunity to fall in love with her.

Jennifer's nerves were on edge before her first audition in front of the judges. She managed to stay calm as she soulfully sang an Aretha Franklin song, but her mood changed to wild excitement as she rushed out to tell her family she had made it to the next round in Hollywood.

Learning About Music

American Idol is all about having audience members decide who is deserving of a $1 million record contract by tuning in twice a week to cast votes in support of their favorite singers and, also, to see who gets voted off. Along the way, audience members are given an insider's look at the hard work and dedication that go hand in hand with landing a music career. Simon has said,

> **"I think we've made all of America into music critics. They know about bad pitch and singing sharp or flat."**

He has also described the show as a soap opera; it has suspense, glamour, a constantly changing plot, and even a villain.

FAMOUS FOR BEING BAD

Simply trying out for *American Idol* made William Hung a celebrity. The Chinese American's version of the Ricky Martin hit song "She Bangs" was so awful that everyone at home watching him had to wonder what he was thinking.

But the cheerful William, a civil engineering student at the time, became a fan favorite anyway—at least for a little while—as he stood his ground when Simon Cowell said, "You can't sing, you can't dance, what do you want me to say?"

William calmly replied, "I already gave my best and I have no regrets at all." Even so, he got a recording contract, had Web sites dedicated to him, made the rounds of talk shows, was poked fun of on *Saturday Night Live*, and appeared in several movies.

Donna Reynolds, in her book *Idol Thoughts: Season Three*, describes the appeal of *American Idol* this way:

> **"The show gets enormous ratings because viewers really care about these people. . . .**

This is why the audition shows work and why the finalists have such strong early support. Viewers feel as though they have been on the journey themselves and take their favorite's success or failure very personally. That investment grows as the competition progresses and reaches a fever pitch during the final weeks. Win or lose, we internalize the results and become part of the experience. "

Summer Replacement Show

By the time Jennifer auditioned for *American Idol* it was a ratings **juggernaut** for Fox Television. The concept for the show had come from England, where its creators, Simon Cowell and Simon Fuller, who managed the Spice Girls, had already launched a talent show called *Pop Idol*. They were well aware that many hit shows in Britain also do well in the U.S. Such shows as *The Office*, *Who Wants to be a Millionaire*, and *Dancing with the Stars* are examples of programs that made the leap from England to America.

Still, when Simon Cowell first brought *Idol* to American television executives, *Pop Idol* had not yet proven itself—and Simon had a hard time convincing the networks of its potential. ABC, NBC, CBS, and other networks all turned down the chance to air *Idol*. Simon recalled,

"I was thrown out of one pitch meeting. After 30 seconds, the guy told me to get out. The main thing we were being told was music doesn't work on TV in prime-time. We tried to explain that there's a lot more than music on the show. "

One person who "got it" was Elizabeth Murdoch. She is the daughter of Rupert Murdoch, head of the parent company that owns Fox Television. Elizabeth was a fan of *Pop Idol* and convinced

Simon Fuller of 19 Entertainment brought to America the idea for a talent show like *Pop Idol,* which was airing in England. Although several networks doubted the concept would work, Fox Television proved them wrong when *American Idol* debuted in the summer of 2002.

her father to air the American version as a replacement show in the summer of 2002. Today, there are about 30 versions of the show airing around the world.

Idol Rules

In the earliest weeks of the 20-week competition, the judges listened to Jennifer and the other successful candidates as they performed, weeding out people they thought were the weakest. That left them with 32 semifinalists who were randomly placed in 1 of 4 groups of 8.

Jennifer was assigned to Group One along with Fantasia Barrino, Diana DeGarmo, Marque Lynche, Matthew Metzger, Ashley Thomas, Erskine Walcott, and Katie Webber. The group assignment is critical because contestants within each group compete against each other. Singers would compete on Tuesday nights, and on Wednesdays the results show would reveal who got the fewest number of votes and had to go. Only two people from each group would go on to the final round as would the singers who are lucky enough to be given "wild card" status.

Group One had three strong singers—Fantasia, Jennifer, and Diana. But only Fantasia and Diana were picked by popular vote to move on to the semifinals. Jennifer was eliminated from the show, but only temporarily.

Randy's Wild Card Choice

Jennifer got a reprieve and the chance to sing again during the wild card round, as did all the semifinalists who had washed out. During this round each judge grants one singer the right to stay in the competition. Viewers at home also can vote one singer back in.

Jackson made Jennifer his wild card choice after he raved about her performance of "I Believe in You and Me," a song made famous by the rhythm and blues group The Four Tops. He said,

❝ Yo, man, you get the prize for the best performance of the night, definitely. ❞

With that performance Jennifer made it into the top 12—the finals—inching closer to the end of the competition when only one singer would remain. As a finalist, Jennifer worked with some of the biggest names in recording history, performing their songs before a live audience and getting feedback from the famed artists themselves.

Jennifer received many glowing reviews from Randy, Paula, and Simon and even from guest judge Elton John, who reacted to her singing his song "Can You Feel the Love Tonight" by saying,

❝Jennifer Hudson blew me away. She sends chills up my spine. It was my favorite performance of the whole lot. . . . That voice is astonishing.❞

Fantasia Barrino (left) and Diana DeGarmo were originally part of the same competition group as Jennifer, but only Fantasia and Diana moved on to the *Idol* semifinals. Although Jennifer bravely returned in the wild card round, Fantasia was unstoppable. She went on to win, and Diana was the runner-up.

Jennifer's heart-felt performances during the *Idol* competition impressed guest judges Elton John and Barry Manilow. Although they raved about her versions of their songs, Jennifer was still voted off the show. Some saw racism in the fans' decision; others blamed the weather for knocking out some loyal voters' phone lines.

Voted Off Controversy

Jennifer was one of three powerful African-American singers who performed during season three. The others were Fantasia and LaToya London. Together, the three judges referred to these ladies as **divas**.

During the competition, Jennifer's fans had some nail-biting experiences. Once Simon told her, "I think you are out of your depth . . . because I think there are better singers and performers in this competition." Jennifer finished in the bottom three on three occasions. The third time, she sang Barry Manilow's "Weekend in

New England." Manilow, who was a guest judge, said that Jennifer "took it all the way," but she was voted off the show in what some considered controversial circumstances.

Jennifer is a true Chicagoan and many of her ardent fans are also from the Midwest. Unfortunately, the night Jennifer was voted off, a tornado had knocked out phone lines for much of her home city. Certainly many people who would have voted for Jennifer were simply unable to.

Different Theories

Elton John thought it was a case of racism and said so because all three women who were dead last that night were black.

Ryan Seacrest, *American Idol*'s host and a famous DJ in his own right, had a different theory. He believed that viewers thought Jennifer's performance was so solid that she didn't need their votes. Instead, they may have used their voting power to shore up singers they thought were more vulnerable. Jennifer said,

> **"I never felt it had anything to do with racism because I don't feel like I have a color. Of course I was hurt. Oh, I cried. But clearly God had a greater plan for me."**

In the end, the competition came down to two singers—Fantasia and Diana. The women each sang three songs, including "I Believe," a song written by former *Idol* contestant Tamyra Gray. The next night during the results show it was revealed that a record 65 million votes had been cast and that Fantasia—a self-taught singer, single mom, and member of the "three divas"—was the winner.

There were no hard feelings, and Jennifer, Fantasia, and LaToya remain good friends and supportive of each other's careers.

Although it took six months of auditions to win the part, Jennifer finally was called perfect for the role of Effie in *Dreamgirls*. Critics and her fellow actors agreed, as shown by the many awards she won for her unforgettable performance.

4
Role of a Lifetime

It didn't take long for Jennifer to get over her disappointment about not winning *American Idol*. She soon discovered that the show wasn't just a hit with fans. It was also a showcase for talent who could be tapped by Broadway and film professionals with the power to cast people in important roles.

One of the casting and **film directors** who watches the show is Bernard Telsey. Telsey has cast performers in such Broadway plays as *Wicked*, *Hairspray*, *Rent*, and *Legally Blonde* and for the movies *Sex and the City*, *Across the Universe*, and *Dan in Real Life*. Telsey said,

> **❝I love watching *American Idol* because it's just like going to open calls that I didn't have to organize.❞**

Another film director who also finds *Idol* useful for spotting talent is Bill Condon. When it came time for him to cast a critical role of Effie White in the movie *Dreamgirls*, he asked several female singers from *American Idol* to try out.

Jennifer first heard about the role at a celebration for the top 12 *Idol* contestants. A fan mentioned that Jennifer would be perfect for the *Dreamgirls* role and Jennifer matter-of-factly said,

> **❝Well, if you see anyone involved with it, tell 'em I'm here and I'm ready.❞**

Audition Process

Fantasia and Jennifer were both invited to try for the part of Effie White, and once again the two friends found themselves in direct competition. About 800 other women were vying for the part as well. Of that number only 12 would be offered **screen tests**.

WANTING TO BE EFFIE

Singer-actress Raven-Symoné had her eye on the role of Effie for the film version of *Dreamgirls*, too. Raven auditioned, but did not get the part.

The Atlanta, Georgia, native was born in 1985 and got her show business start playing a toddler on *The Cosby Show* at age three. She also appeared in *Hanging with Mr. Cooper* and later, as a teenager, had her own television show, *That's So Raven*. She was the voice of Monique on the animated television show *Kim Possible* and was featured in *Cheetah Girls*. Raven branched out to films with roles in the *Doctor Doolittle* movies, *The Princess Diaries 2*, and *College Road Trip*.

She also got an early start as a recording artist. Her first album was released when she was eight and a second, more successful effort was released when she was 14. It was called *Undeniable*.

Director Bill Condon (center) and star Eddie Murphy (left) work on the set of *Dreamgirls*. Condon asked several female singers from *Idol* to try out for the role of Effie. He insisted that the part should go to an undiscovered actress and finally chose Jennifer over all the other hopefuls.

The movie's director liked Fantasia but ultimately chose Jennifer. Still, he said of Fantasia, "She is an amazing human being and has an abundance of talent. No one lost. Someone just emerged as perfect."

Yet Jennifer was no shoo-in for the part. It took six months and several **callbacks** before she emerged with the role of Effie.

Told several times that she did not have the part, Jennifer never stopped believing it would be hers. She said,

> **I am a woman of faith, a firm believer in what is meant to be is meant to be, so if that part was going to be mine, it was going to be mine. And I knew that part was meant for me. . . . Then they called in September and said I was completely out of it, and I wasn't being considered anymore. And I said to everyone, 'No, it's still my part. I'm just waiting for them to realize it.' They thought I was crazy. I believed so much that even if they had gone and cast it with someone else, that they would have eventually come back and given it to me.**

A Pivotal Role

Initially, the moviemakers had some concerns about casting Jennifer. For instance, she had never acted in a movie before and had little acting experience. It seemed risky to give a pivotal role to a newcomer who might not be up to the task of carrying the story when she wasn't singing. Director Condon said,

> **The casting of Effie was crucial. If we had made a mistake, it would have been impossible to overcome. It cannot be a star. The audience needs to discover her.**

Jennifer was given two screen tests. The second time in front of the cameras was the clincher. When Jennifer found out that the part was hers she briefly went crazy.

> **I shouted, I hit the floor. I thanked Jesus. I celebrated for 10 minutes, then I said, 'I got to focus.'**

A Dream Cast

By the time Jennifer came on board other big name stars had already been cast in the $70 million film. First to be cast was Eddie Murphy, a comedian who had gotten his start in the 1980s on *Saturday Night Live*, a late-night comedy program that has launched many movie careers. Eddie played James "Thunder" Early, a 1960's era black singer who tours with the Dreamettes, the all-girl black singing group Effie leads. Eddie was a huge fan of the play on which the film was based and had recorded a few music

Jennifer (left) sings and sways in her first-ever film role in *Dreamgirls*. She couldn't believe she was lucky enough to join so many award-winning stars in the cast, including Beyoncé, Eddie Murphy, Jamie Foxx, and Anika Noni Rose.

albums. He had already starred in many movies, including *Doctor Doolittle*, *Shrek*, *The Nutty Professor*, and *The Haunted Mansion*.

Also already in rehearsal were the women playing the other Dreamettes: Beyoncé, who plays Deena, the woman who competes with Effie professionally and romantically; and Anika Noni Rose, who plays Lorrell Robinson, the third Dreamette. Anika was an accomplished actress who had won a Tony Award for her role in another musical, *Caroline, or Change*, in 2004.

SINGER-ACTRESS BEYONCÉ

In *Dreamgirls*, Beyoncé plays Deena Jones, the character who steals Effie's boyfriend and becomes the leader of the fictional girl group, the Dreamettes, under his direction. Like Jennifer, Beyoncé became famous first as a singer.

Born in Houston, Texas, in 1981, she began singing as a child, forming the group that would become known as Destiny's Child when she was not yet 16. Her father was the group's manager and Beyoncé its lead singer. The group put out four albums before breaking up.

Beyoncé is also a Grammy Award–winning solo artist who has appeared in such movies as *The Pink Panther* and *Austin Powers in Goldmember*. She played the real-life singer Etta James in the film *Cadillac Road*.

Among her many honors, she has been named one of *People* magazine's most beautiful celebrities in 2007 and is the first black songwriter to win ASCAP's Pop Songwriter of the Year Award. She has also won the Critic's Choice Award and Golden Globe Award for her song "Listen" in *Dreamgirls*.

Beyoncé is married to singer-songwriter Jay-Z.

Jennifer especially enjoyed working with Beyoncé. She said, "I'm the hugest Destiny's Child fan. In rehearsals, I'm thinking, I'm in a group with Beyoncé? What fan gets that chance?"

Beefing Up

Rounding out the cast was Jamie Foxx, who plays the part of Curtis Taylor Jr., the girls' manager and boyfriend to both Effie and, later, Deena. Jamie won an Oscar for his performance of legendary singer-songwriter Ray Charles in the movie *Ray*. Jamie would later describe Jennifer as "an incredible artist" who is "bold, honest and fearless."

Now that she had the role, Jennifer immediately began preparing for it. She worked with an acting coach and began eating a steady stream of cookies and other high-fat foods to gain 20 pounds because Effie was supposed to be a large woman.

Jennifer (right) was thrilled to work with Beyoncé (second from left) in *Dreamgirls* because she was always a huge fan of Destiny's Child. Although she was nervous at first, Jennifer found all the experienced cast members extremely kind and helpful to her as a new actress.

Jennifer Holliday, like Jennifer Hudson, got her start singing in church. Holliday delighted audiences for four years in the original *Dreamgirls* musical on Broadway. She won Tony, Grammy, Drama Desk, and Theater World awards for her role as Effie.

Jennifer was nervous the first day on the set. She remembered,

"I thought, 'I know they thinkin' why they got this little girl here?' But everyone, really everyone, was so helpful and welcoming and kind."

Beyoncé, who is a terrific dancer, was especially good at helping her learn the required dance steps. Jennifer also had to learn to be more aggressive to play Effie, who has a larger-than-life personality. Condon gave her unusual assignments designed to harness her inner diva. He asked her to show up late, be rude, get mad, and make friends with the anger that all human beings have inside them but rarely let out. Jennifer literally transformed herself into Effie by completely altering her personality while on the movie set.

FILLING JENNIFER HOLLIDAY'S SHOES

Jennifer Hudson first became aware of Jennifer Holliday's version of "And I'm Telling You I'm Not Going" when she heard the song on an episode of the TV show *The Fresh Prince of Bel-Air*. Jennifer made it her business to learn more about Holliday and her music and decided she would love to sing the song on Broadway someday.

Holliday was the original Effie and won a Tony Award for Best Actress in a Musical and a Grammy Award for the role in the play that debuted the same year Jennifer was born. Effie was Holliday's second Broadway role; the first came when she was just 17 in *Your Arms Too Short to Box with God*. Two years later, Michael Bennett, the director of the Broadway play *Dreamgirls*, cast Holliday as Effie after seeing her in the earlier play. Holliday played Effie for four years before moving on. She also appeared on Broadway in *Grease* and *Chicago* and recorded several albums.

Like Jennifer, Holliday got her start singing in church, and her original Broadway assignment came after she was heard performing at her family's church by a Broadway executive.

Jennifer's passionate ballad, "I Am Telling You I Am Not Going," in *Dreamgirls* brought many audiences to tears. To get into the emotions of the part, she identified with Florence Ballard, whose sad life inspired the character of Effie. Jennifer was also told to channel her anger at being rejected on *American Idol.*

Identifying with Effie

Jennifer says, "I knew I was born to play Effie. Nobody can tell her story better than I can." Jennifer personally identified with Effie as she researched the story of Florence Ballard, the late former member of the Supremes, the 1960's all-girl group on which *Dreamgirls* is based. In the film the character of Effie is based on Ballard, whose life was tragically cut short by alcoholism and heart disease. Ballard was the original leader of the group that became the Supremes but was replaced by Diana Ross when their manager decided Ross would be more appealing to white audiences. Ballard became disheartened, less reliable, and was eventually asked to leave the group.

Jennifer recalled,

"In reading [about Ballard] I got angry for Florence. Like highly upset. Like, ooh, and I felt like her voice."

She was also able to summon her own feelings of rejection she experienced on *American Idol* when Simon told her that she had no chance of winning the competition. Jennifer funneled all of that emotion into her performance of the movie's best known musical number, "I Am Telling You I Am Not Going."

Simon Apologizes

Unlike Ballard, the fictional Effie gets the respect she craves in the movie. And so has Jennifer, who received an apology from Simon. When she was nominated for the Oscar for *Dreamgirls*, Simon said,

"I feel that my criticism has had a significant impact on your career because the buzz on you is huge and I heard your version of 'I Am Telling You I Am Not Going' today. And I would like to be the first to eat a massive dose of humble pie because there are good performances and occasionally there are extraordinary performances and that was extraordinary."

In addition, Jennifer heard from her idol Whitney Houston who attended a benefit in which Jennifer sang "I Am Changing" from *Dreamgirls*. Whitney was so impressed by what she heard that she came up to a stunned Jennifer and said, "You're the one! You! Are! The One!"

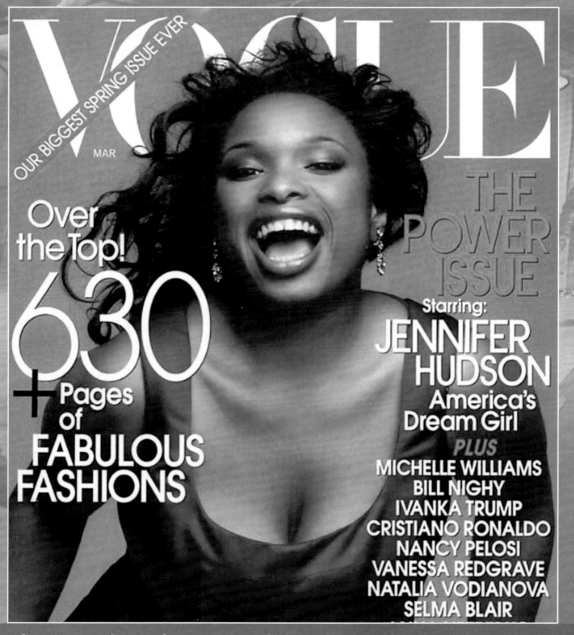

VOGUE

OUR BIGGEST SPRING ISSUE EVER

MAR

Over the Top!

630
+Pages of FABULOUS FASHIONS

THE POWER ISSUE

Starring:
JENNIFER HUDSON
America's Dream Girl

PLUS
MICHELLE WILLIAMS
BILL NIGHY
IVANKA TRUMP
CRISTIANO RONALDO
NANCY PELOSI
VANESSA REDGRAVE
NATALIA VODIANOVA
SELMA BLAIR

After *Dreamgirls*, Jennifer's career reached new heights. She appeared on several magazine covers and won Soul Train, BET, Teen Choice, and NAACP Image awards. She is an inspiration to women of all sizes because she seems so comfortable with herself and her sense of fashion.

5

In a Very Good Place

Jennifer's success in *Dreamgirls* led to a recording contract with the legendary producer Clive Davis, who has worked with two of Jennifer's idols Whitney Houston and Aretha Franklin, along with Justin Timberlake and other superstars. Davis decided to sign Jennifer to a recording contract with his Arista label after he heard her *Dreamgirls* audition tape.

The record contract was inked in 2006, but it took several years before the public got a chance to listen to Jennifer's debut album. In the meantime the singer and actress continued to increase her public exposure in other media. In February 2007 Jennifer appeared on the cover of *Vogue* magazine.

This was a remarkable honor for Jennifer for several reasons. She is only the third African-American woman to appear on the cover of the fashion magazine—the other two were Oprah Winfrey and Halle Berry—and the first African-American singer given that honor. In addition it was also a tribute to how far in the fashion world Jennifer had come after her early days tussling with Simon Cowell over the clothing she had chosen to wear on *American Idol.*

The photograph for the magazine cover was taken by Annie Leibovitz, who is known for photographing some of the biggest celebrities of the day. Said *Vogue*'s editor, Anna Wintour,

> **[Hudson's] happiness in her own skin is something we can draw strength from. The question of body image is a current one, and I can't think of a more compelling and beautiful argument for the proposition that great fashion looks great on women of all sizes than the sight of Hudson in a Vera Wang dress on the red carpet.**

More Honors

A few months later, Jennifer received another honor: she was made a member of the Academy of Motion Picture Arts and Sciences. That means she now has a vote in deciding who the future Academy Award contenders will be.

Other honors came to her in 2007. She received the Soul Train Sammy Davis Jr. Award for Entertainer of the Year, Best Actress and Best New Artist from BET (Black Entertainment Television), and Teen Choice Awards for best dramatic movie actress and outstanding new artist. Meanwhile her hometown of Chicago paid tribute to her with a Jennifer Hudson Day, on which Mayor Richard Daley called her an inspiration. Jennifer used the occasion to tell her fans, "Not only can I do it, but you can do it, too."

In August 2008, Jennifer appeared at the Democratic National Convention in Denver, Colorado, where she sang the national anthem at the request of Chicagoan and then–presidential candidate Barack Obama. Jennifer worried that she would get too emotional singing before an audience of 80,000 people, including the first black candidate to ever receive a major party's nomination for the presidency. Jennifer's mother advised her to get her tears out of the way before the performance, and Jennifer was dry-eyed as she sang before Obama accepted the nomination at the outdoor event in Denver's Mile High Stadium.

Jennifer proudly sings the national anthem at the 2008 Democratic National Convention in Denver, Colorado. She was honored to be asked to perform by Barack Obama, the first African American to be nominated for (and later win) the presidency.

The Secret Life of Bees

Like many African Americans Jennifer was proud to vote for a black man for president—particularly after she got a history lesson that came as part of her second movie role, a non-singing part in *The Secret Life of Bees*. The movie is set in 1964 after the passage of the Civil Rights Act, which made it illegal for businesses, schools, restaurants, hotels, stores, and other public places to discriminate against people because of their race. The movie's plotline also moves into 1965, when the Voting Rights Act eliminated literacy tests often given in the southern states to keep African Americans from voting.

The Secret Life of Bees, which premiered in October 2008, is based on a bestselling novel of the same name by Sue Monk Kidd. *Bees* tells the story of a young white girl named Lily, played by actress Dakota Fanning, who runs away with her caregiver named Rosaleen, played by Jennifer, after Rosaleen is beaten up while trying to vote. Lily and Rosaleen are given a place to live by three sisters played by Queen Latifah, Alicia Keys, and British-Nigerian actress Sophie Okonedo.

To help these talented actresses understand their roles, movie director Gina Prince-Bythewood asked them to read books and watch documentaries about the era. The director also went one step further to immerse the actresses in a time when simply going to the store was a challenge for an African American.

The director instructed Jennifer and Dakota, to visit what they thought was a real-life small-town diner and dollar store in North Carolina, where the film was being shot. The actresses were told to have lunch and buy 10 items. Jennifer quickly discovered that Dakota, who is white, was given better treatment while she was treated rudely and accused of stealing. Jennifer reacted with outrage as anyone would today and only later discovered that the rude store clerks were actors hired by the director to help her get in character. She said,

❝It put us back in the time to see how I would have acted. I would have been arrested or beaten.❞

Jennifer's role in *The Secret Life of Bees* took her back to an era of prejudice against African Americans. She felt angry when she learned more about this treatment of blacks and realized she would have fought hard against discrimination if she had lived during that time.

The Web site *Salon* wrote, "Hudson gives us a Rosaleen who's likable and stubborn, the kind of woman who can get pretty much anything done if she sets her mind to it." And a movie critic for the *Orlando Sentinel* wrote, "Hudson starts living up to her *Dreamgirls* Oscar with a subtle turn here."

Sex and the City

Jennifer also appeared as a new character in the movie adaptation of the *Sex and the City* television series along with series regulars Sarah Jessica Parker, Cynthia Nixon, Kim Catrall, and Kristin Davis. Jennifer played Louise, an assistant to Parker's Carrie Bradshaw character.

The *Sex and the City* movie was made four years after the show ended and updates the lives of the female characters known for their love of fashion and obsession with men. Jennifer is younger than the actresses from the series; her casting was meant to give younger audiences a character to care about and, for the first time, a black character to which to relate.

Jennifer plays an assistant to Sarah Jessica Parker in the movie adaptation of *Sex and the City*. Jennifer's character was added to attract younger audiences and more black viewers. Critics said she made the most out of a small role and enthusiastically praised her acting and singing.

Fox News said Jennifer was terrific in her role, bringing diversity to the story, while the *New York Daily News* described her small role as "pivotal." A reporter for *Variety* wrote,

> **As for new blood, Jennifer Hudson drops in as Carrie's new assistant, graced with a 20-something's faith in love. The *Dreamgirls* star makes more of the sketchy part than she has any right to (and, naturally, belts out one of the songs), while not incidentally representing a demographic break from the show's largely monochromatic palette.**

Winged Creatures

Jennifer also signed to play a role in *Winged Creatures* along with Dakota Fanning, Kate Beckinsale, and Forest Whitaker. Like *Bees*, *Winged Creatures* is also based on a novel. It focuses on what happens to a group of strangers who witness a shooting. The movie went straight to DVD, bypassing theaters.

Jennifer sees all of the small non-singing roles she has taken as learning experiences. She said,

> **I don't want to just do musicals. I want to experiment and do different things and exercise that acting muscle. I'm a firm believer in using what God gives you to make your living. Singing is Number One, and now it's singing and acting.**

Debut Album

Her debut album, *Jennifer Hudson*, took about a year to record and produce. The album shows Jennifer's range from gospel to rock 'n' roll and contains songs from both *Dreamgirls* and *Sex and the City*. Jennifer worked with a lot of artists. They included Robin Thicke, Timbaland, Rock City, Tank and the Underdogs, Diane

Warren, and Ne-Yo. Jennifer was happy that the album reflected so many sides of her. She said,

> **❝It is risky, because people expect you to be one thing. I'm going to take the chance and show what else is a part of me. ❞**

NE-YO WRITES FOR JENNIFER

More than 200 No. 1 records have been associated with *American Idol* stars. Jennifer Hudson's "Spotlight" single from her *Jennifer Hudson* album has been No. 1 on both the rhythm and blues and hip-hop charts. The song, which is the second *Idol*-related effort to reach the top of rhythm and blues and hip-hop charts, was written by Ne-Yo, whose real name is Shaffer Smith. In addition to working with Jennifer, Ne-Yo has penned hits for Beyoncé and Rhianna.

Ne-Yo started writing songs when he was a teen and records his own songs on the Def Jam label. Of Chinese, African-American, and Puerto Rican descent, he earned his nickname when a friend suggested that he reminded him of the character Neo in the *Matrix* movies.

The lyrics for "Spotlight" talk about a woman who is not happy living in the shadow of her man. Jennifer filmed a music video for the song that has been in wide release on music channels.

To promote the album Jennifer filmed a "Spotlight" video that took nearly an entire day to complete. In fact, the filming wrapped at nearly 5 o'clock in the morning. Someone else might have found the experience to be a grind but not Jennifer. She said,

> **❝I loved every minute of it because that's what I dreamed of doing. I used to practice my little moves for my videos in the mirror in my room, with a brush in my hand. I was going to live up every single minute of those 22 hours. ❞**

Jennifer is surrounded by busy assistants before a video session for her single, "Spotlight," from her debut album. Although it took almost a whole day, Jennifer was energized by the experience. She was thrilled to have one more way to fulfill her dream of performing.

Family Tragedy

One of Jennifer's greatest moments—the release of her new album and the critical praise that followed—was marred by a personal tragedy that forced her to cut short her promotion efforts. Jennifer's 57-year-old mother, Darnell; seven-year-old nephew, Julian; and 29-year-old brother Jason were murdered in their Chicago home. Jennifer's brother-in-law, who was Julian's step-father, has been charged with the murders.

Words of sympathy for Jennifer and her family poured in from across the country. Even the Obama family issued a state-ment. Among the mourners at the funeral for the slain family members, held at family's church, were record producer Clive Davis, Oprah Winfrey, and Fantasia, who sang a solo, "Your Grace and Mercy." Jennifer managed to lift her voice in song with the congregation.

Jennifer's mother had always been one of her biggest supporters, and the close-knit family suffered an incalculable loss. It took months before Jennifer recovered enough to resume her work schedule, but when she did she remarked that she was "in a good place" and that performing "was like therapy" for her.

Emerging from Her Grief

Jennifer made her first public appearance after the tragedy at the Super Bowl, where she sang the national anthem. A short time later she appeared at the Grammy Awards as both a performer and an award recipient. About her performance at the Super Bowl one reporter wrote,

> **In her first performance since the slaying of her mom, brother, and nephew, Hudson delivered a crisp, forceful rendering worthy of goose bumps—a take that will go down as the best since Whitney Houston in 1991.**

Jennifer belts out the national anthem at Super Bowl XLIII. Critics praised her rendition as one of the best ever. Soon after that, her fans got to see her again in a powerful performance at the Grammys, where she won the Best Rhythm and Blues Album award for her debut album.

Limitless Future

In her late twenties, Jennifer has a lot of time to flex her acting and singing muscles. She also plans a marriage to David Otunga, who appeared on the reality television show *I Love New York 2*, where he was known as Punk. David, also from Chicago, is a law school graduate who attended Harvard University in Massachusetts. David proposed to Jennifer on her birthday, and the couple has indicated that they have set the date for their wedding, but they have not shared it with their fans to preserve their privacy.

They like to be silly together and enjoy taking bicycle rides with one of Jennifer's small dogs coming along for the ride in her backpack. Jennifer plans to design her own traditional wedding gown and is thinking about having her dogs—Dreamgirl, Oscar, and Grammy—be a part of her wedding party. Before David, Jennifer dated James Payton, her longtime Chicago boyfriend.

Jennifer's future in acting and music continues to be very promising. She credits *American Idol* for preparing her to accept new challenges. The young singer-actress refuses to place limits on herself and confidently looks forward to expanding her abilities and opportunities for years to come.

GRAMMY AWARD WINNER

In February 2009, Jennifer received the Grammy Award for Best Rhythm and Blues album from Whitney Houston. She beat out Al Green, Eric Benet, Boyz II Men, and Raphael Saadiq with her maiden effort that included a version of *Dreamgirls'* "And I'm Telling You I'm Not Going."

At the award ceremony Jennifer said,

❝I would like to thank God who has brought me through. I would like to thank my family in heaven and those who are with me today.❞

She sang "You Pulled Me Through," an album cut that seemed the perfect choice for Jennifer who had just emerged from her family tragedy.

Many reviewers found her debut praiseworthy. A critic from *Vibe* magazine wrote,

❝The gold nuggets in Hudson's first showing are triumphant, womanly anthems. 'Invisible' and 'You Pulled Me Through,' which sanction Hudson's ascending, magnetic vocals, are two wonderful examples.❞

In 2009, Jennifer was invited back to sing on *American Idol*. This time, she came as a Grammy and Academy Award winner singing a song from her debut album.

It was a fitting stop for Jennifer who frequently goes back to her days on *Idol* for inspiration when facing a difficult assignment. She freely admits that being on *American Idol* prepared her to take on anything. And as she looks to her future, she says,

❝I want to continue to sing and act, to write music, to get into charity stuff. I like to do things just for the experience. When I get older, I'll be able to tell my grandchildren that I did *American Idol* at 22, won my first Academy Award at 25 and on and on. I look forward to expanding myself, because I don't believe in limits.❞

1981 Jennifer Hudson born on September 12 in Chicago.

1988 Sings solos in the church choir.

2001 Cast in musical *Big River*.

2003 Auditions for *American Idol*.

2004 Makes it into the top 12; is voted off on April 21 in 6th place.

2006 Films *Dreamgirls*.

Signs record deal.

2007 Wins an Academy Award for *Dreamgirls*.

Appears on the cover of *Vogue*.

2008 Becomes engaged to David Otunga.

Sings national anthem at Democratic National Convention.

Mother, brother, and nephew are murdered.

Secret Life of Bees premiers.

Sex and the City premiers.

2009 Self-titled album is released.

Wins a Grammy award.

Tours with Robin Thicke to support debut album.

Winged Creatures is released on DVD.

Albums
2009 *Jennifer Hudson*

Hit Singles
2009 "Spotlight"

Films
2006 *Dreamgirls*

2008 *Sex and the City*

The Secret Life of Bees

2009 *Winged Creatures*

Awards
2007 Golden Globe for Best Performance by an Actress in a Supporting Role in a Motion Picture

Screen Actors Guild Award for Best Supporting Actress

NAACP Image Award for Best Supporting Actress in a Movie

British Academy of Film and Television Arts Award for Actress in a Supporting Role

Academy Award for Best Performance by an Actress in a Supporting Role

Soul Train Sammy Davis Jr. Award for Entertainer of the Year

Black Entertainment Television Awards for Best Actress and Best New Artist

Teen Choice Award for Choice Movie Actress: Drama

2009 Grammy Award for Best Rhythm and Blues Album for *Jennifer Hudson*

NAACP Image Award for Outstanding New Artist, Outstanding Duo or Collaboration for "I'm His Only Woman," and Outstanding Album for *Jennifer Hudson*

audition—Opportunity for actors and others to show what they can do in hopes of getting a role they desire.

Broadway—Street in New York City where most major live theater is performed, although any major production in New York is regarded as a Broadway play.

callbacks—Invitations extended to actresses or actors to read for roles more than once.

church elder—Leader in a Christian church.

critics—Journalists who comment on the artistic merit of films, music, theater performances, and other forms of the fine and lively arts.

divas—Extraordinary female singers often deserving of and insisting on special treatment.

film director—Artistic head of a film production.

juggernaut—Huge force, campaign, or movement that crushes anything in its path.

rhythm and blues—Form of music that was a forerunner of rock 'n' roll, combining elements of jazz and blues; developed mostly by black performers.

screen tests—Filmed tryouts often in full makeup and costume to determine if an actor or actress is right for a particular part.

soprano—Female voice capable of singing notes in the highest pitch.

Books

Rich, Jason. *American Idol: Season 3 All Access*. Roseville, CA: Prima Games, 2004.

Walsh, Marissa. *American Idol: The Search for a Superstar*. New York: Bantam Books, 2002.

Periodicals

Gardner, Elysa. "Hudson Makes No Secret of Her Goals: Singer/Actress 27, Looks Forward to a Long Career." *USA Today* (September 29, 2008): p. D-4.

Hinkley, David. "Jen's Singing Was Super, So Don't Give Her Lip." *New York Daily News* (February 4, 2009): p. 71.

Karpel, Ari. "The New Girl in Town." *Entertainment Weekly* no. 992-993 (May 23, 2008): p. 56.

Moody, Nekesa. "Jennifer Hudson's Old Dream and Music Now a New Dream." *Pittsburgh Post-Gazette* (October 3, 2008): p. C-6.

Norment, Lynn. "A Moment in Time." *Ebony* vol. 64, no. 1 (November 2008): p. 72.

Smith, Ethan. "How a Reject from American Idol Became Hollywood's New Dreamgirl." *The Wall Street Journal* (December 14, 2006): p. B-1.

Web Sites

www.americanidol.com
> *American Idol*'s official Web site includes information on the current season's contestants, including episode recaps, a map showing where the contestants live, and about *American Idol*'s charity, Idol Gives Back.

www.dreamgirlsmovie.com
> Official Web site for *Dreamgirls* provides information about the cast, a movie trailer, and the original play.

www.foxsearchlight.com/thesecretlifeofbees
> Official Web site of *The Secret Life of Bees* contains information about the cast, a movie trailer, videos, a director's blog, and recipes.

www.jenniferhudson.com
> Jennifer's official Web site includes her biography, photos, videos, news, and tour information.

www.sexandthecitymovie.com
> Official Web site for the *Sex and the City* movie features videos, trailers, cast biographies, and photographs.

page

2: Kaye Evans-Lutterodt/NMI	**32:** DreamWorks/NMI
8: AMPAS/PRMS	**35:** DreamWorks/NMI
11: AMPAS/PRMS	**37:** DreamWorks/NMI
13: AMPAS/Zuma Press	**39:** DreamWorks/NMI
14: Splash News and Pictures	**40:** PPRS/NMI
14: (insert) Fox Network/PRMS	**42:** DreamWorks/NMI
16: Fox Network/PRMS	**44:** Vogue/NMI
19: Tim Cammett/KRT	**47:** Bradley Lail/USAF
20: Fox Network/PRMS	**49:** Fox Searchlight Pictures/NMI
23: Fox Network/PRMS	**50:** New Line Cinema/NMI
24: Fox Network/PRMS	**53:** Arista Records/NMI
27: 19 Entertainment/NMI	**55:** Kevin Dietsch/UPI Photo
29: Frank Micelotta/Getty Images	**56:** Arista Records/NMI
30: Fox Network/PRMS	

Front cover: Steve Granitz/WireImage
Front cover insert: Fox Network/PRMS

ABOUT THE AUTHOR

Gail Snyder is a freelance writer and advertising copywriter who has written more than 15 books for young readers. She lives in Chalfont, Pennsylvania, with her husband Hal, and daughter Ashley, and listens to rock 'n' roll music whenever possible.